Print information available on the last page

Rev. date: 06/10/2016

To order additional copies of this book, contact:
Xlibris
1-888-795-4274
www.Xlibris.com
Orders@Xlibris.com

Contents

BIBLE CITATIONS

Scripture quotations marked NKJV are taken from the New King James Version.

INTRODUCTION

Drug addiction is an evil, despair filled circumstance and something I didn't ever think I would ever experience. Additionally, drug addiction is a destroyer of dreams as well as happiness. The first time I tried any drug I was instantly addicted. My reality was denial and denial led me into a deep, dark depression. Believing I was in control of my marijuana addiction, I thought that trying harder drugs like crack, cocaine, meth and heroin wouldn't be a big deal. I have never been more controlled than under the influence of crack-cocaine. Little did I know how powerful crack was and other hard drugs. The dark path I was walking for years became darker. This darkness that was pure evil brought me to the brink of death. Satan wanted my soul. I ended my first book writing, "God's love has saved me and his love can save you as well." This book is the story about that statement. There is hope for the addicted and the people walking in darkness.

Mathew 4: 16, the people living in darkness have seen a great light and, those living in the land of the shadow of death a light has dawned.

Acts 9: 1-30, the story of Saul

This book is dedicated to my dad, Robert Butler, who passed away September of 2015, of Parkinson's disease. Also, I would like to dedicate the book to the addicted, depressed and anxious. Finally, my calico cat Ophelia, who was the only one with me during my darkest hours. I had to put my little girl down the summer of 2008.

CHAPTER 1
FREEDOM

The summer of 2006 I was released from the Arizona probation department after successfully completing the program. Regaining my freedom came at a cost though. The lawyer fees and all the fines totaled an estimated $10,000, not to mention the small fortune I spent on crack-cocaine after becoming addicted in 2004.

I was very fortunate that the state of Arizona passed a law just a handful of years before my arrest on March 1, 2005 which enabled me, a first time offender, to go to rehab instead of prison. If the law wasn't in place I would have gone to prison, surely. Likewise, if I had not completed probation I would have gone as well. God gave me the strength to stay clean, sober and out of trouble, during my probation. Thank you Lord.

Gaining back my freedom, that I had taken for granted, meant I could once again leave the state of Arizona. In 1998, I bought a timeshare which is not the smartest thing to do, like smoking crack. The thing is, if you do fall into that trap and don't use it then it really makes no senses at all. My decision was to visit

Hawaii and the island of Kauai was the only island available in September. I had been there in 1990, so I knew the island a little bit. Kauai is so beautiful. It really is paradise on earth. It is known as "The Garden Island", because it is so lush and colorful. The shades of green are amazing. I had just survived hell on earth so, being there was quite ironic. My good friend Kookie, took care of my sweet orange, brown, black and white calico cat Ophelia for me while I was away.

Kauai was more beautiful than I remembered. Probably because I had a clear head, that visit. When I was there in 1990 I had been addicted to pot for six years and cocaine for about three years. And yes, that trip in 1990, I found some buds. I knew I could get it this trip as well but, I was so tormented and terrified about what I had been through that I stayed away from the crap. The trauma you experience during an addiction like that is horrifying.

The trip was quite lonely because the way I felt after the arrest. The isolation I punished myself with was oppressively sad. I drank beer, watched football and went to the beautiful beaches to relax. One day I went boogie boarding at a beach whose tempestuous reputation preceded it. As I was floating in the turbulent ocean I got caught in a rip tide. It's a scary thing. After what seemed like an eternity splashing helplessly, I was exhausted. I could not hang on any more. The waves crashed over me, I was swallowing a lot of salt water and was losing the struggle. I thought to myself, "If I'm going to die why not in paradise?" I was drowning. Then, a peaceful feeling came over me and it was like someone pushed me from behind. Instantly out of nowhere, I was able to touch the bottom of the ocean and keep my head above the salty water. There was no one around as I dragged myself to the beach and collapsed. I know now it was the hand of God. It wasn't my time to leave planet earth yet.

CHAPTER 2

FAMILY

When I got back from Kauai, I knew I had to see my family back in the Midwest. Narrowly escaping death once again, I felt my chances were running out. Since my crack addiction and subsequent arrest, I had not seen them for about three years. My dad had survived prostate cancer and now was dealing with Parkinson's disease. I felt terribly, having not been around the last few years. Actually, drug addiction to weed and coke took me away from my family years before.

Backing up before the arrest, in 2005, out of college I moved to El Paso, Texas. I taught seventh grade math there for the next thirteen years. Talk about cheating death. I should have died a hundred times there. I did so much coke my nose would bleed at a good flow. It would hurt so badly I would ice it down after I got it to stop bleeding. Then, back to the enticing powder. I learned to free base coke (for smoking) so I wouldn't have to snort anymore. After snorting one line my heart would feel like it was going to explode.

I've always had low self-esteem but after my arrest it hit a new low. Thanksgiving was coming, so I decided to go up to Iowa to reunite with the family. Following years of tradition, the Iowa Hawkeyes and

Minnesota Golden Gophers played football that weekend in Minneapolis. It was the first time I've been to that game during the holiday and a great time to see the whole family after so many years.

My dad always planned the trip the weekend of that particular football game. He looked forward to it so much. Making plans for his family and friends gave him a lot of joy. He was very kind, a 6'4" gentle giant. He was the travel agent for that game. He was loved by so many and the best dad. (One quick story: Dad used to drive a school bus. He apparently would let dogs on the bus so they wouldn't get run over. After he retired, I guess that stopped and the dogs were in danger.) It was great seeing Dad and everyone else again. I lost it when I saw my nieces and nephews. I broke down in tears. I didn't think I would ever see them again. They are such special children. All you have to do is read one of my children's books and you would know.

CHAPTER 3
BACK TO THE DESERT

After the holiday was over I returned to Mesa. The last year or so I had been renting a room at a house in Mesa, AZ. It was a house turned into just bedrooms, bathrooms, and a kitchen with laundry room. There were seven tenants, each of whom had struggled with alcohol and other drugs. We all had our own problems. One of the rules was no drugs so, that's why I choose the place. Turned out it wasn't true. I could tell shortly thereafter that the land lady didn't really care. Still and most importantly for me, there was no crack there while I was on probation.

I met a lot of interesting people at that house. Some were really cool, good people but others, not so much. One of the good ones was a dude that went by the nickname, Chief. He was playing guitar in his room one time, so I walked down to check it out. There we became friends and, he introduced me to a terrific woman, Kookie. We are all still good friends. Chief is quite the guitar player. During my stay at the house in Mesa, I began writing poetry which I had never done before. With this new friendship, my poems turned into lyrics for Chief's music. Before we knew it, we had written thirteen songs. We started a band that we called, "Black Algae Days". We had fun, played a few gigs and that's about it. We could never find a consistent bassist and drummer. The two of us had a lot in common. The love of rock and roll was one of them. It turned out that one of our favorite bands was Led Zeppelin. It was a fun time.

After probation was over, a couple of crack heads moved into the house. Thank God it was after I was out of probation because I did break down and smoke the last few months of 2006, as I remember. All it did was bring back some terrible memories and agony. I was starting to freak a little because I was having a hard time stopping. It was terrifying thinking of what would happen if I was arrested. If I would have gotten arrested again, I would have gone to prison. I used what I learned in rehab and was able to break the chains of crack addiction and haven't smoked since. Also, I could see that the second-hand smoke was killing my precious Ophelia.

CHAPTER 4
THE CLUB

The end of January of 2007, I escaped from the crack laden house and was able to stay with some guys I knew. Turned out they were smoking meth, so I got out of there and got my own place. It was time to find a job. I knew a friend of a friend that worked at a night club. By the end of February, I was working the parking lots as a security guard, showing people where to park and collecting money since we all worked for tips. At the end of the night we would pool the money together and split it up.

The club was a hip-hop club and could get a little rough at times. The people that frequented the club were drug dealers, gangsters and other criminals. A small percentage of people that came to the club weren't from those categories and ranged from working class folks to professional athletes. There were a few fights to break up from time to time. Now and then there would be a weapon. One night, we had to take somebody out of the club by force. Later, after we closed for the night and as we were walking the girls to their vehicles, there was a drive-by shooting. As I waited at the door, a car pulled up. I turned to look at it and the window went down and someone in sun glasses started shooting at the club. I hit the dirt and yelled, "Gun gun, get down!" By the time some of the guys came from the back lot, with guns drawn the car was gone. It happened so fast. I was just glad nobody was hit by a bullet.

It was a tough job having to be on our feet for nine to ten hours. That was the worst part. We couldn't sit or we'd get in trouble. The shoes were very, very important. There were a lot of bad attitudes walking around but you had to be cool in order to collect tips, the remnants of the gangsters' blood and drug money. One night when I was in the front lot a car drove up to me. There were a few guys in it who asked if I wanted to make a little extra money selling coke. I'm an addict not a drug dealer. I wanted no part of hard drugs, not using anymore and absolutely not selling them.

After about seven months I was promoted to bar-back. This meant more money and also more responsibility. The main thing all the time was security but now I had to take care of the bartenders and make sure they had everything they needed. They were great young ladies, pretty, and very good at what they did. There was a strict rule about dating the girls so I didn't. I would have but I needed a job, so I couldn't take the chance. I know some guys did but, I was afraid of losing the job. Also, I felt like a dirt bag because of the arrest in '05. It really never crossed my mind that a pretty girl there would want anything to do with me. I was still punishing myself. I felt like I deserved to die alone. A few more months went by and I was promoted to manager. The problem with that is there is nowhere to go but down in that business.

Things were going well until one day I noticed a lump in Ophelia's neck. I took her to the vet and it turned out to be cancerous. I knew it was from the second hand smoke of the pot and crack, so I blamed myself. I had to have her put down. It was my fault that she was gone now. I killed her! I was devastated

It was wild walking into a park, sitting down and smoking a joint. After a while I'd get up and continued the journey.

Another thing we did was kayak the canals. It was really cool. We joined a gym close by. We would work out then grab a kayak and cruise the canals. So beautiful seeing the city's architecture, and people sitting at cafés next to the canals. Also, the trees and other scenery were stunning, and going under the bridges was joyous as we floated down the canal. I went to a couple of concerts when I was there as well. Two of my favorite bands were playing in the country so, I took a couple of adventures.

The first concert I went to was Alice In Chains. They were playing in the city of Eindhoven. I took the train to the southeast part of Holland and got a motel room. After I got checked in I found a coffee shop and went in to chill before the show. AIC was really good but no Layne Staley, the original lead singer. He died of a heroin overdose back in 2001. The next day it was back on the train and back to Utrecht.

The second concert I went to was The Cult. That show was in Den Hague. When I got to the city I knew the general location of the arena but, it was a few miles away so, I had to go on a discovery walk unlike in Eindhoven. After a few hours walking all throughout the city looking for the venue I found it. I asked a few people along the way but, they weren't a lot of help. I had looked at a map back at the apartment, so I had an idea where it was located. It was a great show and after I couldn't find any hotels so, I caught the train back to Utrecht. I made it to Amsterdam as well. Jimmy had a friend that lived above the "Red Light District" there. Free will was everywhere. Well, that summer came to an end like all others so, it was back to the USA and my new home, for the time being, Kansas City, Missouri.

CHAPTER 6
MELISSA AND NICOLE

I got back to Kansas City at the end of August. Summer was over so, as far as I was concerned it was my last one. Spending the summer in the Netherlands was my, I guess you could say, last hurrah. A friend of a friend worked abroad for the government and was out of town. They needed someone to watch the house, so I had a place to stay. What I was going to do was stay there through the end of the year and then make my way to Texas.

When I got to the states, I found out my parents were having a bit of a financial crisis. Well, that confirmed my thoughts of committing suicide. I was going to house sit to the end of December, go spend Christmas with my parents one last time, and then head to the Gulf. It was perfect. I was going to leave my folks all that I had left. Since I had disgusted so many people with my crack addiction and arrest, at least I could do something good before I left this place, help out my parents.

Since life was ending, I started to drink heavily and smoked pot when it came around. That's how I spent the months before going back to Iowa for Christmas. December 3rd came around first, which is a special day for my family and I, especially my sister. It was my niece's birthday. She came into our lives via adoption. What a joy she has been.

The next day was the 4th of December and started out like any other day. Sometime during the day I got a phone call from a friend that lived in Phoenix. The news wasn't good, instead it was heart-breaking. Two bartenders that I had worked with at "The Club" were found murdered that morning. Turns out it happened some time the night before, they were strangled to death. To this day there still has been no arrest. What happened was nobody had heard from them for a while, so a friend went over to the house where they were living to check up on them. When she got to the front door it was locked. There was no answer when she knocked on the door. She went around back to see if they were on the deck. When she got there, they weren't there. Looking in the back window, she saw a lifeless body one the floor. She called the police after that terrible discovery. I can't imagine how she felt.

Nicole Glass was a blonde haired little fire cracker. She was so spunky and always smiling. I can still hear the words she said to me one night. She said, "Dave, you are spicy!" I smiled and said, "Well, how about that and you're spicy too." Melissa was a cute, fun little senorita. She intimidated me with her persona. I don't think I hardly talked to her for the year and half I worked with her. An autopsy revealed that Melissa was eight weeks pregnant when she was killed. So, not only did these jerks kill two sweet young ladies they killed an innocent child as well. Now, if the door was locked when their friend went over there it tells me they must have known the killer(s). There was no forced entry, so they were probably let in. This injustice has gone on long enough. Please check out their story and bring awareness to this despicable crime!

The thing that hurts is I think Melissa, Bebe, had a crush on me. If she did, I surely didn't think a 25 year old beauty would want anything to do with a forty something year old dirt bag. I always felt that Jesus put me there for a reason. Maybe it was to get them away from that life style and the club they worked at. After I found out the news I sobbed for weeks. I kind of blamed myself for not doing something more when I worked there. It was more fuel to end my life!

CHAPTER 7
GRACE

On December 22nd, I went back to Waukon, Iowa to spend my last Christmas with the folks before heading to Texas. Because of what happened to my two friends in phoenix, I was distraught and ready to implement my plan of suicide. I felt as if I failed another time in this life and didn't deserve to live anymore. I didn't deserve to be loved. I had screwed up enough and it was time to leave.

The next day was December 23rd and I was still quite upset. Many emotions were flowing through me. That night I went to one of the restaurants in town and took a seat at the bar. I had one too many beers by the time I left. When I walked outside it had started to snow at a pretty good clip. The roads were already in bad shape and now they were snow covered. It had probably snowed about a half of a foot. I was thinking to myself that I better be careful driving back to my parents house. I got a DUI five years ago when I was arrested so, if I got another one, I'd probably be going to jail. That was not part of my plan.

Well, I got in the SUV and decided to take the back way home to try to avoid the cops. Waukon has a population of about 4,000 people. There was really no reason to freak out like I did. I could have just walked home, for cryin' out loud. The back road went around the golf course. It's on the south side of town but still in Waukon. I was being very cautious because there was a bend in the road ahead. When I went around the bend I fishtailed and went into a little ditch off the left side of the road that was in front of some houses. I went into the ditch just enough so I wasn't able to get out. It was around midnight so no one was awake in the houses.

I opened up the door and jumped out and the snow was probably up to my waist. I started to freak out a bit I didn't know what to do. Damn, I've been drinking and buzzed. I would surely blow over 0.08! First I tried to push the SUV back. It might have worked if it was in neutral and not in park. It didn't budge. I decided to walk to the house about a half mile away. I left the lights on in the SUV which, probably in hindsight wasn't the best idea. They were shining bright and should have caused some attention.

When I got home I was starting to panic. What was I going to do? It was about 12:30am at that time. My dad had the early stages of Parkinson's disease and my mom was 5'1" so there wasn't anything they could do. Anyway, they were sleeping. As I paced the floor a thought came to my mind. Look up a tow-truck and get pulled out. Even though it's a small town there had to be someone out there that I could call.

The first place I found on the computer I immediately picked up the phone and gave them a call. All I got was a message they were done for the night. The second place I called there was no answer. There was one more number to try, so with fading hope I called it. After a couple of rings someone answered. I had a glimmer of hope. The driver came to the house and we were off to the site of the SUV. Many thoughts were going through my head. What was the situation now and what was going to happen? The lights had to have gotten someone's attention. Did they call the cops, would the cops be at the sight of the SUV? If they were I was probably going to be arrested since I had been drinking and over the legal limit.

We saw the SUV in the distance and thank God there were no police lights. We got to it and there was nobody up at the houses. He hooked up the tow and the SUV was out in a matter of seconds. He followed me home just in case another ditch was in my future. I pulled into the drive way still shaking thinking I was going to be arrested when we got to the vehicle a few minutes ago. I got out and asked how much it was going to be. He said, "Oh, just give me twenty bucks." I gave him a big hug, fifty bucks and went in the house in disbelief. When I got into the house, I fell to my knees in tears.

CHAPTER 8
A BEAUTIFUL LIGHT

When I woke up the next morning, Christmas Eve, I told my parents about the events of the night before. They were disappointed but glad it worked out. My dad, being the kind guy he was, gave me forty bucks. He wouldn't take no for an answer so I accepted it and gave him a hug.

As the day went by I was still quite distraught and upset at what happened the night before, the murders in phoenix and I was running out of time. During the day, at some point I had a talk with my mom. I broke down and asked her, "Wouldn't it be better if I would die? Then you guys could have all I have left." I was going to kill myself anyway, I just needed some reassurance. She didn't agree, of course, but I knew I was going to, nothing was going to stop me. I was at the end to my rope, and I was tired of hanging around.

The family got together for Christmas Eve later in the day. My sister was having Christmas Eve dinner. It was great spending time with my nieces, their faces so full of love and life. At least one was still a believer in Santa Claus. That afternoon I was talking to my youngest niece about Christmas. She told me about the "Elf on the shelf". It was new to me we didn't do that growing up so, I asked her about it. She told me that each night until Christmas day, the elf would move from one place to another.

I questioned her about it teasingly, "That's cool, but are you really sure?" Then, she looked at me and said with a very serious voice, "Oh yes, my friend stayed over the other night and we heard bells!" I smiled, chuckled turned my head and shed a tear. Children are the best, I love them they are so innocent. I thought to myself, "Why is the world so evil and why do they have to grow up?!"

We had decided to go to midnight mass, which was at 10pm. Night fell and off to St. Patrick's Catholic Church we went. It was a packed house when we got there. I don't think we could all find a place to sit together so I just sat in the back row. I kept my eyes closed during mass and my head was bowed down. I started to cry during mass at some point. I think at the start of the scripture, the readings. My tears kept coming, more and more heavily.

Father Joseph Schneider was the priest at that point in time at St. Pat's. It was time for the Gospel and then the homily. My tears continued to roll down my face with my eyes firmly closed. When it was time for the homily the message was about forgiveness and hope. Father Joe started talking about sin and how we all sin, that even he does. I was balling at this point when he said, "Accept God's forgiveness for your sins and become a beacon of hope for others." It seemed like he repeated those words a hundred times. I was still crying with my eyes closed.

All of a sudden, it seemed like someone was talking right in my ear to the right of me. The voice got my attention and I thought, "Man, he's been saying that for a while now," it was almost hurting my ears. I lifted up my head with tears running down my face, and looked at Father Joe. I was a bit startled because it seemed he was looking right at me with a deep stare. Then I noticed a light coming from above and he was glowing, the light was so bright it was radiant. It seemed that rays of lights were shooting out and up from him. As I followed the cylindrical light up to the ceiling of the church, it sparkled with gold and silver particles it seemed. My eyes went wide open and my jaw dropped to the ground. I noticed something in the bright light but not sure what. It startled me again. Then a smile fell over my face and I felt a powerful energy rush in me. All the negative thoughts of suicide were gone. I didn't know what I felt, dang, I had no idea what I had seen even, but I was changed somehow. Without noticing, the light was gone as I kept smiling and wiping the tears from my face. Again, I had no idea what I had witnessed but it was a beautiful light that was positively breath-taking.

CHAPTER 9
REBORN

After seeing the light I was changed. The shame, despair and guilt I felt from being arrested, leaving school that day in 2005 because I needed to buy crack, was gone. It felt like a big weight had been lifted from me. I felt joyous! It felt like I was loved. It's really hard to explain.

Like I had mentioned before, I started to write. After my arrest I wrote a poem/story and made sure I kept track of it for the next five years or so. Something told me to write down the words, so I did. The story was what I called, "A Day At The Park With Friends".

A Day At The Park With Friends

Josh, Amelia, Sydney, Fifi, Sassy and Sky went for a walk one day they looked for a park to play

When they finally found one oh boy did they have fun there were slides there were swings they glided as if they had wings

They had so much fun playing in the sun going round and round up and down

When they were done having so much fun some thugs came to them they had some drugs

The friends looked each other in the eye they remembered what their uncle said, "Try drugs and you could be dead."

Uncle Said he loves us very much and doesn't want us to do that stuff don't be influenced by someone bad he said this because he had

Uncle said he tried them and drugs made him sick he didn't think they were that bad now he wishes that he had

He said, "Scream and run away!" Then go tell mom and dad they would be very proud they would be glad now when the friends go to the park they will know how to react if someone offers them marijuana, heroin, meth, cocaine and crack

When I got back to Kansas City I started going to church every day in the morning. I was longing to figure out what I had seen and why things seemed so different. One day I was thinking about the story and the part that went, "Scream and run away!" I knew if children would ever read that it would scare them so, it had to be something else. One day I thinking about those words asking myself, what could it be? A thought came to my mind and it was, "YELL NO! LET'S GO!" So I changed, scream and run away to yell no lets go. That was it …Yell No! Let's Go!

When I relocated to Kansas City back at the end of the summer of 2010, my parents had told me about a girl named Jenn. I was going to walk into the ocean never to be seen again, I wanted to die. I wanted nothing to do with her or anyone else for that matter. My mom had been bugging me about it for four months so I decided to give her a call sometime in January. January came and I gave this Jennifer a call. I left a message and didn't get a response. A few weeks past and my mom called me and informed me that I was going to get a call from Jenn. I said, "What? Who?" and she said, "You know the girl you called and left a message." Apparently, Jenn got the message but lost the number. She called a mutual friend of her and my mom's and got my number from her.

A week or two passed and then I got the phone call. It was Jennifer and we talked for a while. We decided to meet the upcoming weekend for a burger and karaoke. I had heard she could use a friend, some rotten things had happened to her and she was a little blue. Well, I was too until I saw the light. We hung out and became friends. That's all it was to me and her I'm sure, we were just two lost souls hanging out.

One day I told her about what I had seen and she wasn't the first one I told. I was looking for answers, I was confused. Jennifer was converted to Catholicism, she was born Southern Baptist. My point is she knew a lot about the bible and me being a cradle-catholic, I don't think I ever picked one up. She showed me the story of Saul in a bible. I didn't know what the story was about, I didn't have a clue. I read it and I started thinking about the light. Then, Jennifer said to me, "Do you know what you saw?" I said, "Jesus?" Then she replied, "No, you've seen the light of the Holy Spirit."

EPILOGUE

Jennifer and my friendship turned into something more than we both ever expected. I started, the process of trademarking, YELL NO! LET'S GO! I secured the mark the following year and started the book project. On August 8th, 2012 Jenn and I were married in Waukon, at St. Pat's by Father Joe. Since that amazing day I have written many more children's books and have had three children's books published. Also, I have written a book about the story that led to my arrest, in 2005. It is, "Through The Eyes of Ophelia: A Story of Addiction". The prequel to this book.

Since I've witnessed the light of the Holy Spirit, I have seen some amazing things as well. For instance, I have been outside on a sunny day and it has gotten so bright that I am blinded to the point of only seeing right in front of me. I have had to kind of feel my way back into the house so I could see again. Another thing is one afternoon I was outside and the thought came to me to take a look in the back yard. There's a SUV in and under the car port so, I walked around until I could see the yard. Well, my favorite bird is the Cardinal and to my amazement when I looked back there, the yard was covered in red. There were as it seemed hundreds of male Cardinals. I was stunned. I stood and watched them for quite some time, then walked to the back to see if it was real. As I got the back they all took flight and I stood there in wonder.

One more story I would like to tell you about is one evening Jenn and I were sitting on the bench out front. I looked to my left and noticed what looked to be a cat sitting on the other side of the car kind of peering out. I said something trying to get its attention and then it walked out and came towards us. We were a bit surprised, the cat was a gold color and longer than a yard it seemed. It looked like a little bobcat as it walked towards us. The large cat got to us and then rubbed and bumped against us. I think I picked it up, under its front legs, and gave it a kiss. It was so long and big but so very gentle. I put the little bobcat back down and turned and gave Jennifer a kiss. After we kissed I looked at her and smiled, I couldn't believe how big that cat was. We turned our heads to look at the cat again and it was gone. We walked to the cars and looked under them. There was no cat, so, we walked around to the back and looked but, no cat. It was quite unbelievable, almost angelic.

Before I had the children's books published the name Christopher David came to my mind, so I decided that would be the pen name that I would use when I published my children's books. My first book, "Through the Eyes of Ophelia: A Story of Addiction", the children's books, and this book are available on my website and also through Xlibris publishing.

I will speak to anyone that will listen to me about what I witnessed and how a crack addiction nearly killed me. With me, I will hopefully bring some hope to you. My website is www.yellnoletsgo.com

God bless

Printed in the United States
By Bookmasters